To Elijah ("my God is YAHWEH"):

May you forever walk in the Way!

But we have this treasure in jars of clay to show that this all-surpassing power is from God and not from us.

II Corinthians 4:7 (NIV)

www.mascotbooks.com

The Adventures of Clayoton: Clayoton Meets the Potmaker

For more information, please contact:
Mascot Books
560 Herndon Parkway #120
Herndon, VA 20170
info@mascotbooks.com

Library of Congress Control Number: 2016913178

CPSIA Code: PRT1016A
ISBN-13: 978-1-63177-766-0

Printed in the United States

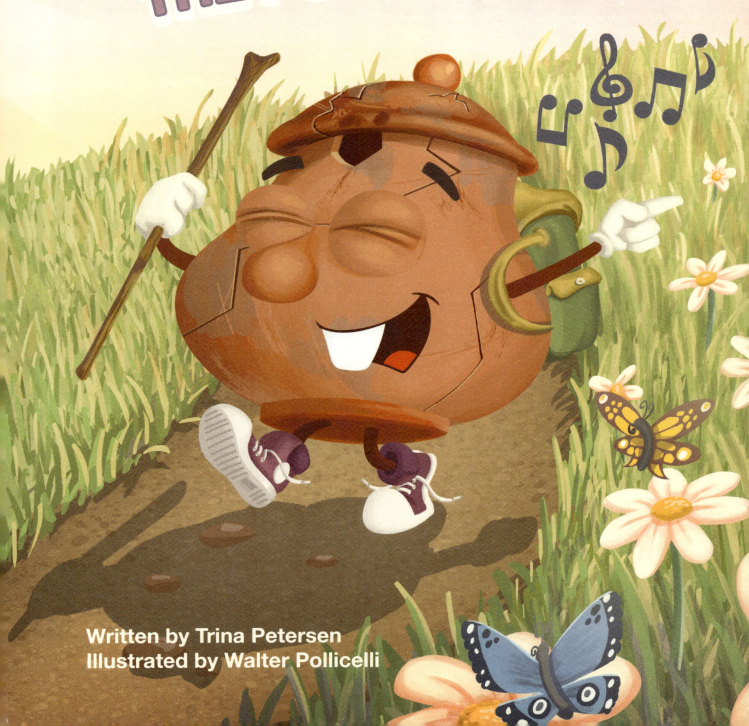

THE ADVENTURES OF CLAYOTON
CLAYOTON MEETS THE POTMAKER

Written by Trina Petersen
Illustrated by Walter Pollicelli

Far away, nestled deep in the land of Candor, there was a kingdom named Vesselicity. It was not known for fancy cars or video games. And, though there were many, it was not known for its party places or toy stores. Vesselicity was known for one thing only: its pots.

That's right. Vesselicity was a kingdom full of pots made in every shape, size, and color. There were kettle pots, coffee pots, cooking pots, and washing pots. Some were tall like trees and others miniature like bushes. There were golden pots and silver pots. Some pots were round and others skinny like string beans.

The king of Vesselicity was of a very different kind. He did not sit on a throne in the kingdom. Instead, his throne was atop the highest mountain, way up in the clouds. No one had seen him, but some pots claimed to have heard his voice.

There was a STORY told in Vesselicity that said the king promised to return one day to inspect the pots. Any pot he found to be a treasure would be taken to the highest mountain and placed in a showcase made of glass. The pots he did not approve of would be thrown into a big, fiery oven.

Some pots believed this story, while others did not. But there was one pot in particular who was very concerned. His name was Clayoton.

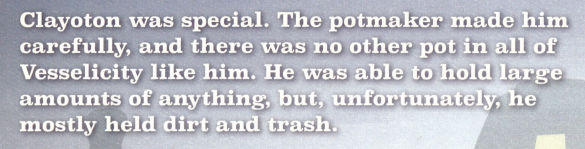

Clayoton was special. The potmaker made him carefully, and there was no other pot in all of Vesselicity like him. He was able to hold large amounts of anything, but, unfortunately, he mostly held dirt and trash.

Clayoton often looked around the kingdom to admire the beauty of other pots. *Why didn't the potmaker give me anything fancy?* Clayoton thought. *I just want to look special too.*

Clayoton had been used a lot, so he was shabby, dull, and had many scratches and chips. He worried he might be thrown into the fiery oven when the king came. Clayoton did not think of himself as being valuable or a treasure. This made him very sad.

I KNOW! Clayoton thought excitedly. *I'll visit the potmaker. I'm sure he can change me into something special.*

He was surprised to find the potmaker left written directions on how to get to his throne. *If the other pots in the kingdom can hear the potmaker's voice, maybe the potmaker can hear mine.*

So, Clayoton went outside and shouted, "I'm coming to see you, potmaker! I'm tired of being chipped and broken. I need to know if you can make me into a special pot."

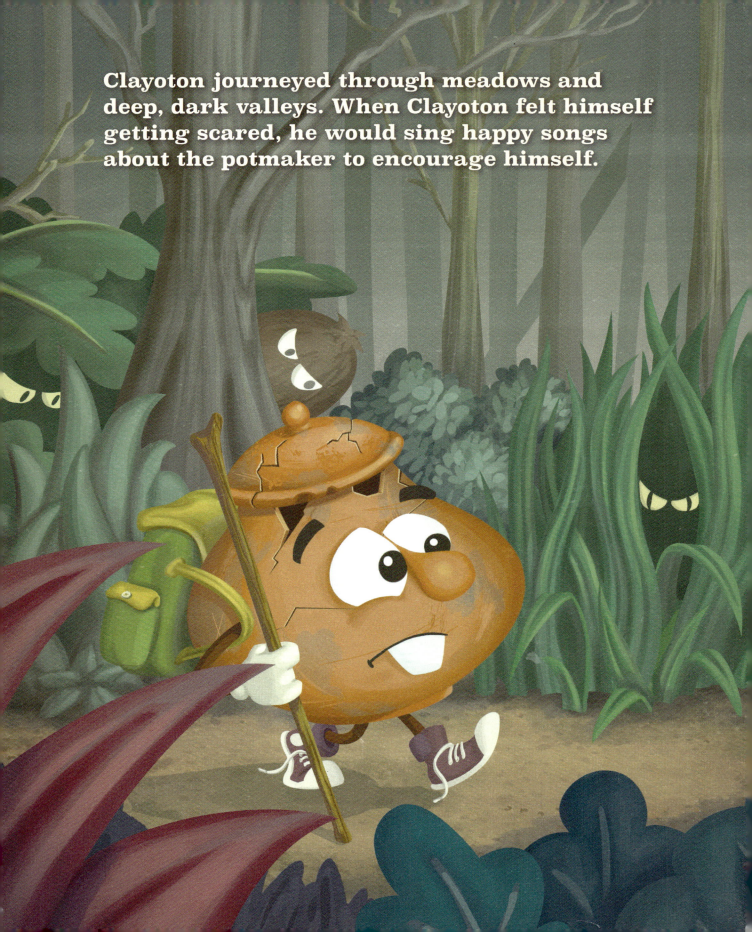

Clayoton journeyed through meadows and deep, dark valleys. When Clayoton felt himself getting scared, he would sing happy songs about the potmaker to encourage himself.

I sing as I walk through the valley in the dark,
For I'm going to see the king who will fix my chips and marks.

He will repair my cracks and restore my broken piece. So I will
walk through the valley past the shadows, past the beasts.

Even though Clayoton was scared and lonely, he was determined to find the potmaker. One day, when Clayoton was very tired, he stopped to rest. He missed being in Vesselicity with the other pots. It was so quiet here Clayoton could hear himself breathing and thinking.

"Clayoton," a voice whispered. "Clayoton."

"WHO SAID THAT?" asked Clayoton.

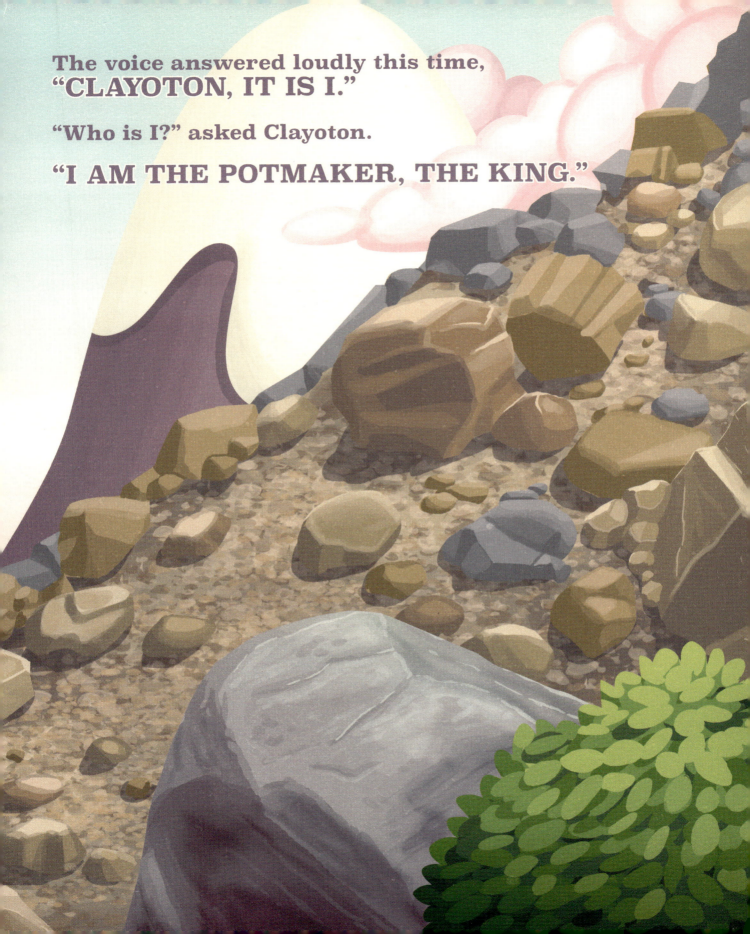

The voice answered loudly this time,
"CLAYOTON, IT IS I."

"Who is I?" asked Clayoton.

"I AM THE POTMAKER, THE KING."

Clayoton looked around, under, up, and down, but Clayoton did not see anyone.

"THE POTMAKER?!" exclaimed Clayoton. "The potmaker who made me?"

"Yes," said the voice, "I am the real potmaker, the king. I am the potmaker who made you, Clayoton."

Clayoton was excited but also scared. None of the pots he knew had ever talked to the potmaker. "Do not be afraid, Clayoton. I have been waiting for you."

"Waiting for me? How did you know I was coming?" asked Clayoton.

"You told me! I listen when you talk to me! You are one of my **special** pots."

Clayoton could not believe it! The potmaker had just called him special. "I don't feel special," said Clayoton. "I am not shiny or tall. I don't have jewels or gems, and I don't have a fancy top."

The potmaker spoke softly, "Listen to me, Clayoton. When I made you, I made you special. **Sparkles, shine, jewels, and gems don't make you special.** And having a fancy top doesn't make a pot special."

"Well if those things don't make a pot special, what does?" asked Clayoton.

The potmaker's words were gentle. "What makes a pot special is not how it looks on the outside. **What makes a pot special is the treasure it holds on the inside.**"

Clayoton was very confused. "The only things people put in me are dirt and trash. Do you have treasure you'll put in me? Will you fix my broken piece?"

Clayoton's question made the potmaker very happy. "I have already given you what you asked for. As you journey home, you will experience the changes I made. And, Clayoton, you don't have to travel so far to talk to me. You can talk to me anytime you want."

Clayoton was happy to hear this. "This is a long way to travel. I had to pass through the Valley of the Shadow of Dark. How can I talk to you if I don't come here?"

The potmaker smiled. "Clayoton, is it true that though you cannot see me you can hear me?"

"Yes."

"Remember this," said the potmaker. "You can talk to me anytime. I am always with you, and I always hear you. All you have to do is get quiet enough to hear me."

"**WOW!**" exclaimed Clayoton.

He never dreamed he would talk to the potmaker and receive a treasure. Clayoton felt full and happy as he traveled home. He sang a happy song.

I believe the words the potmaker spoke.
He made me special and now I have hope.
He fixed my crack and restored my broken piece,
And the treasure he gave will help my joy to never cease.

Clayoton couldn't wait to get back to Vesselicity! He would tell the other pots of his decision to meet the potmaker and fears as he walked through the Valley of the Shadow of Dark! And, although he had not seen him, Clayoton would tell the others the potmaker was real and how he spoke with him and could feel his love!

I will tell them any pot can talk to him any time. They only need to get away from the bumping and clanging of Vesselicity, Clayoton thought happily.

CLINK! CLINK! CLINK! Clayton felt warm and began to glow! He had never felt so happy or full before!

The potmaker's promise was true! Clayoton thought. He had received a treasure—the first of many!

ABOUT THE AUTHOR

Trina M. Petersen is the author of *Rise Up O Daughters of Zion: Good Morning! Great Day!* and the artist of *First Fruits*—a poetic offering. She obtained Bachelor of Arts in Biblical Education and a minor in Christian Counseling from Beulah Heights Bible College and a Master of Divinity from the Interdenominational Theological Center, both located in Atlanta, Georgia. Having overcome issues of low self-esteem and feelings of worthlessness by the power of God, she is determined to make a difference in the lives of men, women, and children by helping them build Christ-centered self-esteems.

Have a book idea?
Contact us at:

info@mascotbooks.com | www.mascotbooks.com